## DATE DUE

KALEIDOSCOPE

# WATER

by

Roy A. Gallant

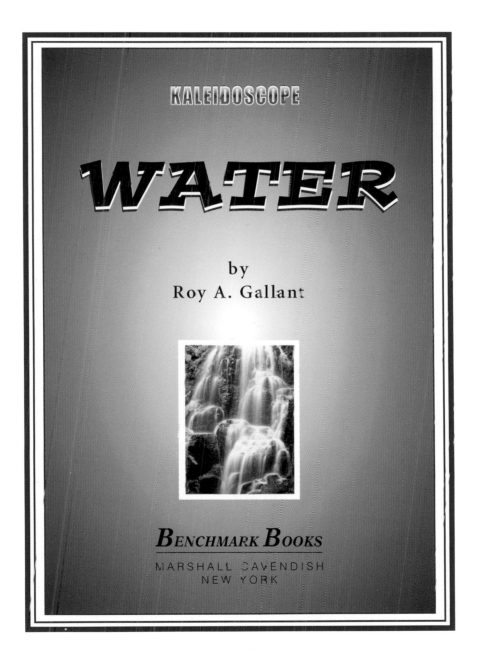

*B*ENCHMARK *B*OOKS

MARSHALL CAVENDISH
NEW YORK

Series consultant:
Dr. Edward J. Kormondy
Chancellor and Professor of Biology (retired)
University of Hawaii-Hilo/West Oahu

Benchmark Books
Marshall Cavendish Corporation
99 White Plains Road
Tarrytown, New York 10591-9001

Library of Congress Cataloging-in-Publication Data
Gallant, Roy A.
Water / by Roy A. Gallant
    p. cm. — (Kaleidoscope)
Includes bibliographical references.
Summary: Explains why water, although common, has characteristics which make it an unusual substance.
ISBN 0-7614-1040-6
1. Water—Juvenile literature. [1. Water.] I. Title. II. Kaleidoscope (Tarrytown, N.Y.)
GB662.3 .G35 2001     551.48—dc21          99-049627

Photo research by Candlepants Incorporated

Cover photo: Corbis / Clark Mishler

The photographs in this book are used by permission and through the courtesy of: Corbis: Clark Mishler, 5; Jim Sugar Photography, 18; Michael S. Yamashita, 37; Douglas Peebles, 42. Photo Researchers: © Petit Format/Nestle/Science Source, 6; Mehau Kulyk, 9; © Calvin Larsen, 10; © Scott Camazine, 13; © Ronald E. Royer/JPL, 14; © Bill Bachman, 17; © Charles D. Winters, 21; © Paolo Koch, 25; © Engelbert, 26; © Stephen Dalton, 29; © Larry Cameron, 30; © Lawrence Migdale, 33; © Garry D. McMichael, 34; © Dennis Flaherty, 38; © Kazuyoshi Nomachi, 41.

Printed in Italy

6 5 4 3 2 1

# CONTENTS

# AN UNUSUAL SUBSTANCE

Water is everywhere. It covers almost 70 percent of Earth's surface. It forms the oceans and flows as rushing rivers. The atmosphere—not to mention clouds—is a vast storehouse of water in the form of the gas called *water vapor*. Billions of tons of water are locked up as the enormous ice caps that sit on the top and bottom of the world. If all of that icy water were to melt, it would cause a rise in sea level of about 260 feet (80 meters). Coastal cities the world over would be flooded beyond repair.

*Near the poles, most of the water is in the form of ice. This huge frozen wall is part of Alaska's ice sheet system.*

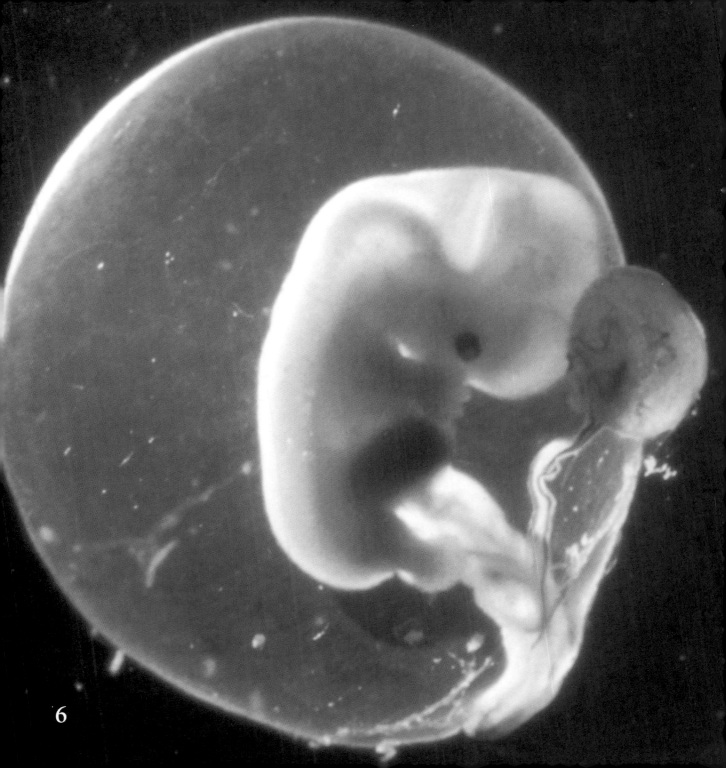

6

You yourself are about 70 percent water, with a few bones tossed in. But even your bones are 22 percent water. Before you were born you developed in a safe, warm pool of water inside your mother. Indeed, all life on our planet depends on the precious liquid. Animals and plants alike could not survive long without it.

*This human embryo will spend about nine months in a sac of watery fluid inside its mother.*

If water is so common, why is it also unusual? It is the only substance on our planet that can exist as a liquid, a solid, or a gas. Water is constantly changing shape. Freeze water, and it becomes ice. Boil it, and it turns into steam. It is also unique because of its role as a *universal solvent*. This means that water can dissolve, or break down, just about anything.

Like a sculptor, water carves solid rock into strange, often beautiful, shapes. That was how the Grand Canyon was formed over millions of years and how miles of limestone caverns were sculpted deep underground.

*An ice cube melts into water at the same time it evaporates as vapor into the air. Three states at the same time—one of the traits that makes water so unique.*

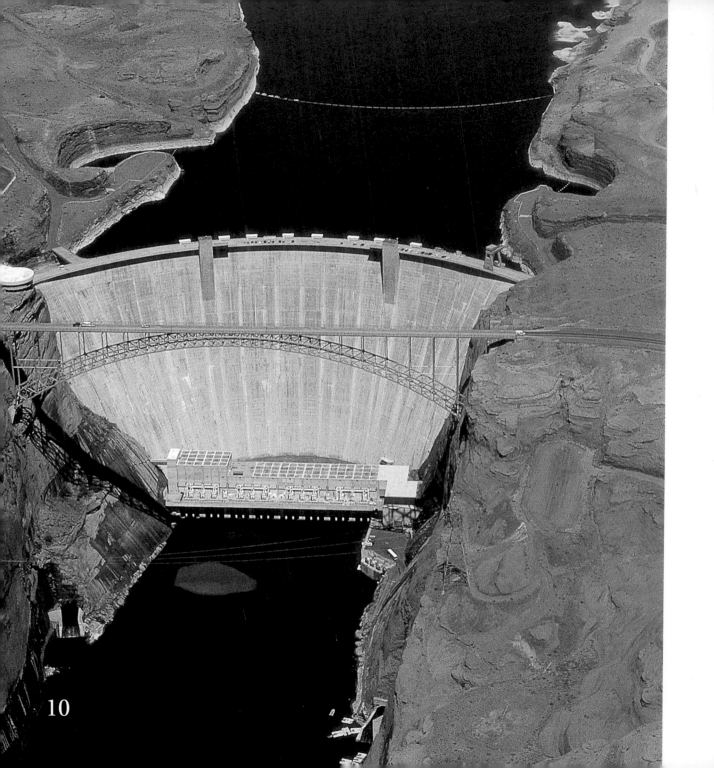

But with the power to dissolve stone, it is easy to see how water can be harmful as well. When floodwaters surge across the land, in only a few hours buildings can be washed away and farmland destroyed. But when locked up behind huge dams, water turns the machines that make electricity to light our homes and run our factories. We swim in it, ski on it, and use it to move goods and people all over the world. Water touches our lives in so many ways it would be hard to list them all.

*Huge dams, such as Arizona's Glen Canyon Dam, hold back rivers. The blocked water then turns the blades of turbines, which create electricity.*

# THE BIRTH OF WATER

Earth's water originally came from two main places: volcanoes and comets. Soon after the birth of our planet, about 4.5 billion years ago, volcanoes poured gases into the newly forming atmosphere. One of the main gases was water vapor. Cooling in the upper air, the vapor formed liquid droplets that fell as rain. After millions of years of volcanic action, the rain collected as ponds, flowed as streams and rivers, and began to fill up the ocean basins. Today 95 percent of Earth's water is locked up in its rock crust. Only about 5 percent is "free," and 99 percent of that water is in the oceans.

*The smallest possible "piece" of water is a molecule. Each one is made up of two hydrogen atoms (green) joined to one oxygen atom (red).*

13

14

While the oceans were forming, storms of comets rained down onto our planet as well. Comets have been described as "dirty snowballs" because they are made up almost entirely of ice and space dust. This ice was added to Earth's store of water. One new theory states that showers of these cosmic snowballs continue to fall, adding water vapor to Earth's atmosphere. They weigh from 20 to 40 tons each and can be as large as a house. If this is true, then Earth's supply of freshwater is increasing at a rate of some 3 trillion tons every 10,000 years.

*In the past—and maybe even to this day—icy comets have been a source of Earth's supply of water.*

However, many scientists say there is not enough proof for such a claim. They feel that the planet's supply of water has stayed nearly the same over the past millions of years. As it is, that adds up to a very big glass of water. If we poured all of Earth's water into a cup, it would be 700 miles (1,120 kilometers) long, 700 miles high, and 700 miles wide.

*Millions of gallons of water help create these falls in south-eastern Australia.*

# WATER WAYS

By far most of Earth's water is stored in the ground. And most of it is so far down that it will never make it to the surface in our lifetime. It is locked up in the tiny spaces within solid rock. Or it is the water that was trapped in sediments when they were turned into stone. Still more of it is part of the molten magma, or liquid rock, that is in and underneath Earth's crust. Only after several million years, when that solid rock decays, or when magma wells up to the surface as lava, is this water freed.

*From time to time in Earth's long history, volcanoes have added large amounts of water vapor to the atmosphere. They still do to this day.*

Most of Earth's water supply is in slow motion. Water at the surface *evaporates* and enters the atmosphere as water vapor. Most of that vapor comes from the oceans, but some comes from trees and other plants. Their roots take in water from the ground. At the same time, the leaves release water that enters the air as water vapor.

As it rises into the atmosphere, this warm, moist air—heavy with water vapor—starts to cool. As it does, the vapor *condenses* into the fine water droplets we see as clouds. When enough of these tiny droplets collect, they become heavy enough to fall out of the cloud as rain. Sometimes they cool so much that they fall as snow or hail.

*The leaves of green plants make their own sugary food out of sunlight. As they do, they give off vapor, here seen clinging in little bubbles.*

21

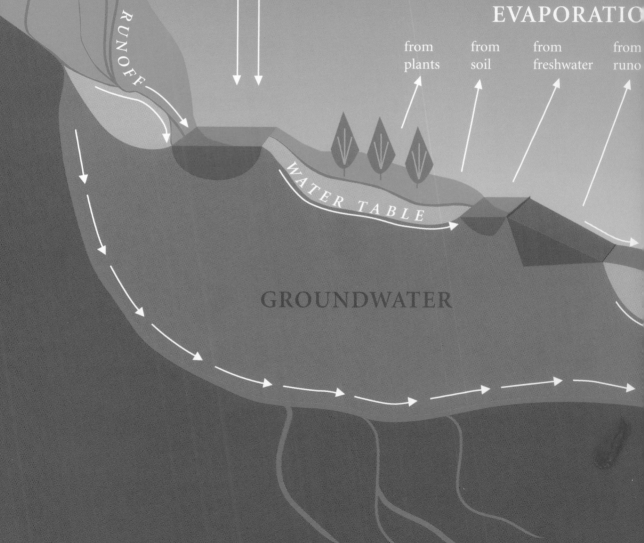

**PRECIPITATION**

RUNOFF

**EVAPORATIO**

from plants

from soil

from freshwater

from runo

WATER TABLE

GROUNDWATER

When the liquid water reaches the ground, some soaks in, some evaporates again as water vapor, and some flows back to the sea as rivers and streams. While about 40 percent of rainwater and melted snow flows into the sea as runoff, the remaining 60 percent is returned to the atmosphere again as water vapor. Those are world averages, though. The *water cycle* is much different in regions such as rain forests or in deserts such as the Sahara.

*Earth's water cycles endlessly. It evaporates from the surface as water vapor. The vapor then cools in the upper air, condenses, and falls as rain, snow, or hail.*

23

Energy from the Sun is the driving force behind the water cycle. Heat affects the water cycle in important ways. In hot and moist regions, such as the rainy Tropics, the water cycle is more active.

Large amounts of water vapor rise off the warm tropical oceans. Droplets form in the atmosphere, until the clouds are bursting with rain. The wettest spot in the world is Cherrapunji, India. In one four-day period 100 inches (254 centimeters) of rain fell.

*When the monsoon season arrives in India, it seems to rain without end. Moist air rising off the Indian Ocean feeds the monsoons, often causing floods.*

Compare that with the driest spot in the United States— Greenland Ranch, Death Valley— which has an average yearly rainfall of less than 1.5 inches (3.8 centimeters). Usually these hot and dry regions are deserts.

*The water cycle is different from region to region. Desert air can be so dry that falling rain evaporates before it hits the ground.*

# WALKING ON WATER

Almost everywhere you go, you are walking above water. About 22 percent of the freshwater that isn't locked inside rocks stays hidden from sight. *Underground water* lies beneath the surface, moving in mysterious ways. That is forty times more freshwater than we can see above ground, not including the oceans.

*This small animal, the Jesus lizard, can actually walk on water with great speed.*

Rainwater sinks into the ground, working its way down through the soil and through cracks in the rocks. This underground water may reach depths of up to 1 mile (1.6 kilometers), but most seeps down only about halfway before it is stopped by hard clay or the solid *bedrock*. This region down to the bedrock becomes *saturated* with water, meaning that it cannot hold any more liquid. All that water is called *groundwater*, and the top level of the groundwater is called the *water table*.

*Alaska's Copper River Delta. As rivers flow into the ocean, they carry large amounts of sediment. Some of this matter piles up and forms a delta, or low-lying plain.*

Earth is like a giant sponge soaking up and squeezing out water. Depending on the amount of rainfall, the level of the water table is always changing. Where the water table is high enough to be at ground level, there is a swamp or a marsh. A basin-shaped hollow in the groundwater zone forms a pond or lake. Streams and rivers start as springs bubbling out of a mountainside or as meltwater from snow. In these ways, much of the water above the bedrock finds its way to the surface and becomes part of the water cycle.

*Water is key to our survival. But as this swimmer knows, water can also mean fun.*

# A THIRSTY WORLD

We all need water to drink. We rely on it in our homes for cleaning, cooking, bathing, and carrying away wastes. We also use it to irrigate crops, to fight fires, to treat wastes, and to make thousands of products.

But do we have enough to go around? It's hard often to get water to the places that need it most. And the world's population grows larger every year.

*The furrow method is being used to irrigate this corn. Small trenches carry water across the field.*

Since the 1950s, our use of freshwater has tripled, but the supply has
stayed the same. The more people,
the more food they require. The
more food, the more water is needed
to grow it.

The result? On all continents
water tables are falling as we take
water out of the ground faster than
the water cycle can replace it. China
and India, with their enormous
populations, are among the world's
most troubled spots.

*Some people actually celebrate water.
This family in Cambodia has brought
their boat to a water festival.*

But these Asian nations are not alone. In the United States, so much water is being taken out of the Colorado River that a mere trickle of the former river ever reaches the ocean.

What about the oceans themselves as a source of usable water? A number of ways of removing the salt from ocean water have been tried. But it turns out to be much too costly to produce large amounts of freshwater that way.

*A horseshoe bend in the Colorado River. When it started looking more like a stream than a river, people grew alarmed.*

Then what does the future hold? Should we be worried about our freshwater supply? Yes, we should. Some areas of the world are seriously parched because of frequent droughts. Others have plenty of water but are polluting it so much that it is too dangerous to drink. Among the major offenders are factories that dump their wastes into rivers and streams, killing fish and making the water harmful to humans. Fertilizers and pesticides also drain off farmlands and poison our rivers.

*In some parts of the world, water is hard to come by. People have to walk for miles to the nearest source. These children in Niger are making sure they don't spill a drop.*

Nature is always reminding us of its life-giving resource: pure mountain streams, bright flakes of winter snow, or the roar of a waterfall. But while we depend on water, water does not depend on us. As long as there is a drop of water and the Sun to send it skyward, the water cycle will keep on quenching the world's thirst. The two lessons we must learn are to conserve and protect the water we have.

*A water-skier sends up a wall of spray.*

# GLOSSARY

**bedrock**   The solid layer of rock beneath the surface.

**condense**   To change from a gas, such as water vapor, to a liquid.

**evaporate**   To change from a liquid to a gas.

**groundwater**   Liquid beneath Earth's surface down to the layer of bedrock.

**saturate**   Fill to the limit; for example, when the soil cannot take in any more water, we say the ground is saturated.

**underground water**   All the water that is below surface level.

**universal solvent**   A substance that can dissolve almost anything, given enough time. Water is also known as the universal solvent.

**water cycle**   The never-ending movement of water as it evaporates from Earth's surface, becomes the gas water vapor, then condenses high in the atmosphere, and falls as a liquid back to Earth.

**water table**   The top level of the groundwater.

**water vapor**   The dry gas water turns into after it evaporates.

# FIND OUT MORE

**Books:**

Charman, Andrew. *Water*. Chatham, NJ: Raintree Steck-Vaughn, 1994.

Cooper, Jason. *Water*. Vero Beach, FL: Rourke, 1992.

Dorros, Arthur. *Follow the Water from Brook to Ocean*. New York: HarperCollins, 1993.

Gibson, Gary. *Making Things Float and Sink: With Easy-to-Make Scientific Projects*. Brookfield, CT: Millbrook, 1995.

Hoff, Mary K., and Mary M. Rodgers. *Our Endangered Planet: Groundwater*. Minneapolis: Lerner, 1991.

Kalman, Bobbie, and Janine Schaub. *Wonderful Water*. New York: Crabtree, 1992.

McLeish, Ewan. *Keeping Water Clean*. Chatham, NJ: Raintree Steck-Vaughn, 1998.

Murphy, Bryan. *Experiment with Water*. Minneapolis: Lerner, 1991.

Oxlade, Chris. *Science Magic with Water*. Hauppauge, NY: Barron, 1994.

Perham, Molly, and Julian Rowe. *Water*. Danbury, CT: Watts, 1996.

Richardson, Hazel. *Water*. Brookfield, CT: Millbrook, 1998.

Walker, Sally M. *Water Up, Water Down: The Hydrologic Cycle*. Minneapolis: Lerner, 1992.

White, Larry. *Water: Simple Experiments for Young Scientists*. Brookfield, CT: Millbrook, 1995.

Wick, Walter. *A Drop of Water: A Book of Science and Wonder*. New York: Scholastic, 1997.

Williams, Brenda. *Water*. Chatham, NJ: Raintree Steck-Vaughn, 1999.

Websites:

Science Activity: It Floats!
homeschooling.about.com/library/blsciact6.htm

Kids Korner: Hands-On Projects & Experiments
saltaquarium.about.com/msub31handson.htm

Water Weights Craft
craftsforkids.about.com/library/projects/blwatwcr.htm

Water Quality around the World
environment.about.com/msubwat2.htm

Drinking Water in the U.S.
environment.about.com/msubwat1.htm

# AUTHOR'S BIO

Roy A. Gallant, called "one of the deans of American science writers for children" by *School Library Journal*, is the author of more than eighty books on scientific subjects. Since 1979, he has been director of the Southworth Planetarium at the University of Southern Maine, where he holds an adjunct full professorship. He lives in Rangeley, Maine.

# INDEX

*Page numbers for illustrations are in boldface.*